Arduino

The complete guide to Arduino for beginners, including projects, tips, tricks, and programming!

Table of Contents

Introduction

Thank you for taking the time to pick up this book about Arduino.

The Arduino technology started as an idea in 2003 by Hernando Barragán to simplify the BASIC stamp microcontroller, and reduce costs for students who wanted to purchase such technology.

Since 2003, the Arduino technology has rapidly expanded from its humble beginnings in Italy, and is now available worldwide in a number of different models.

This book aims to educate beginners on all things Arduino, and will take the reader from a complete novice, to a competent user.

Within this book, you will discover the different Arduino models you might like to choose from, the key terms relating to Arduino, the many functions of Arduino, how to set up your Arduino, how read and write code, and finally, how to use your Arduino to power some cool projects!

Once again, thanks for choosing this book, I hope you find it to be helpful, and enjoyable. Welcome to the incredible world of Arduino!

Chapter 1: What is Arduino?

With the age of technology being in full swing has come an increase in the average person's technological literacy. That is, more and more people are becoming versed in the hardware and software of the modern age, whether as dabbling hobbyists or as professional engineers.

For whatever reason, you and many others have been attracted to Arduino. Perhaps you have seen the variety of projects online or in person that are built on Arduino technologies, or maybe you have heard of the flexibility and ease of building gadgets with Arduino. Whatever the case, you are interested in learning more about Arduino and how to utilize the technology in your own life. First, let us look at what Arduino is and its history.

History of Arduino

The Arduino technology started as an idea in 2003 by Hernando Barragán to simplify the BASIC stamp microcontroller and reduce costs for non-engineering students to purchase such technology at the Interactive Design Institute in Ivrea, Italy. A microcontroller is a small computer board that can be programmed to perform certain functions. At the time, BASIC stamp microcontrollers cost $100 and upward, and, as we will see later, Arduino certainly reduced the costs while maintaining the ability to perform various functions and the ease of programming such functions.

Supervised by Massimo Banzi and Casey Reas, Barragán worked in the computer language called Processing to create the environment, IDE (Arduino's official coding environment and program). He fiddled with the Wiring platform technology to come up with the hardware called ATmega168, the first Arduino microcontroller.

Later in 2003, Massimo Banzi, David Mellis, and David Cuartielles added support for Wiring to their microcontroller board, named ATmega8, and they reworked the Wiring source code, naming it Arduino. Together, the three along with Tom Igoe and Gianluca Martino continued to develop Arduino technologies such that in the year 2013, 700,000 microcontroller boards were sold from the New York City supplier, Adafruit Industries, alone.

After some issues with establishing the trademark for Arduino, which resulted in a split in the company for a few years, Arduino is now a single company that is committed to the development of hardware and software usable by the average person or hobbyist, but also flexible enough to be of interest to the professional engineer.

But what *is* Arduino?

This history of Arduino might sound as convoluted as the technology itself seems to you. Full of so much puzzling and confusing elements, you might feel overwhelmed by the language of "microcontrollers," "environments," and "languages." However, this book is intended to demystify Arduino. We will start here, beginning with the definition of Arduino.

According to Arduino's official website, Arduino is an open-source electronics platform with easy-to-use hardware and software. What this means is that Arduino has created hardware that can be easily built and understood by a non-engineer, as well as software, or a way to code instructions for the hardware, in a similar easy-to-understand way. Both were developed in an open-source model, such that the creators of Arduino do not own the rights to the ideas behind the software and hardware, but instead allow anyone who would like to tinker around with the hardware and software a legal means of doing so.

To explain a few other terms, microcontroller boards are the "hardware" of which the Arduino community speaks, and they are essentially small computers usually good for smaller tasks, not functioning as an entire laptop or desktop computer nor even as a smartphone or tablet. It is, in fact, a "micro" computer.

How it works is as follows: one purchases the hardware that is appropriate to his or her purposes and then, on a more powerful Windows, Macintosh OSX, or Linux computer, codes, or write instructions for, the board and uploads the instructions via a cable. The code is then stored on the microcontroller and it functions according to the instructions, such as turning on a beeping sound when light filters in through an opening door and hits a sensor connected to the microcontroller, like an alarm.

Who Uses Arduino?

A whole array of people uses Arduino for various projects and hobbies, as well as for professional use. It is known for being simple and straightforward enough for beginners, deep and rich enough for the beginner to grow, and with enough potential for a more advanced user to utilize.

Teachers and students use Arduino, and indeed were the intended consumer base for the products, as Arduino offers a low-cost way to build scientific instruments. This allows teachers and students to practice and demonstrate chemistry and physics principles, as well as to get started with programming and building robots.

Designers and architects might use Arduino technologies to build interactive models and prototypes of what they hope to develop on a full-scale. Musicians and artists also use Arduino microcontrollers to experiment with new instruments or techniques in their art.

Just about anyone can use Arduino, including children, to start tinkering with coding and computer hardware, as well as hobbyists who simply want to learn a bit about software and micro computers.

Why Use Arduino?

Arduino microcontrollers have numerous advantages over other, comparable technologies. They were designed to be more flexible, more cost-efficient, and more accessible to the user than their alternatives. As such, Arduino technologies have become a fast-growing competitor to the Parallax BASIC stamp, Netmedia's BX-24, Phidgets, MIT's Handyboard, and many others.

The first advantage was the driving force behind creating Arduino microcontrollers: cost-efficiency. Rather than the $100 that some other boards cost, a pre-assembled Arduino board costs less than $50, and the boards that can be manually put together cost even less.

Second, another positive feature of the Arduino microcontroller boards over other board types is that the Arduino environment, IDE, works across platforms. This means that you can use a Windows computer like any other microcontroller board would probably require, but you can also use a Macintosh OSX computer, or a computer running Linux and work just as easily with the Arduino software. This opens up the use of microcontrollers to the Apple user and the open-source Linux user.

Speaking of open-source, the software for Arduino is open-source, which is a third advantage. The tools, or strings of code that you use to instruct the microcontroller in order to accomplish certain functions, are accessible by anyone. You do not have to purchase a license to use these tools, so teachers can teach students about them and students can learn them without added cost.

Fourthly, the open-source tools are also extendable by the C++ libraries and the AVR-C coding language, meaning that those with more in-depth knowledge of code would be able to benefit from using these technologies as well. There is depth to the software and programming features that allows the more dedicated to go deeper, while being enough of a straightforward coding language to allow the hobbyist to tinker as well.

A fifth feature of Arduino is that the environment in which a person codes for the microcontroller is simple and clear. This means that the computer program, IDE, which you would use to program the instructions for the microcontroller, is straightforward and easy to understand. This makes working with the software a smooth experience.

Finally, the fifth advantage to Arduino is the open-source hardware. Arduino board technologies are published under a Creative Commons license. Anyone who desires and has the knowledge to do so could find and create their own hardware to use with Arduino software programming in the IDE environment. Even those who are not experienced circuit designers can use a breadboard to create their own Arduino circuit-board.

Chapter 2: Key Terms in Understanding Arduino

When working with Arduino technologies, that is, in choosing a board, writing the coded instructions, setting up the microcontroller for use, and finally using the Arduino board, it will be helpful to understand the terminology of Arduino. In this chapter, you will find some key terms that will aide you greatly in your endeavor to become an Arduino user.

As mentioned earlier, Arduino is **open-source**, meaning you can use it and teach it to others without violating any copyright laws. It is based on easy-to-use **hardware**, which is the actual physical computer board with which you will be working, and straightforward **software**, the coded instructions with which you will use to direct the hardware to perform a task of your choosing. Software is also known as **code** and the individual pieces of instructions are called **tools**.

Anatomy of the Arduino Board

The board itself contains a good number of parts. The **digital pins** run along the edges of most Arduino microcontrollers and are used for **input**, or sensing of a condition, and **output**, the response that the controller makes to the input. For example, the input might be that the light sensor senses darkness, that is, a lack of light. It will then close a circuit lighting up a bulb as output: a nightlight for your child.

On most boards, there will be a **Pin LED**, associated with a specific pin, like Pin 13 on the Arduino Uno. This Pin LED is the only output possibility built into the board, and it will help you with your first project of a "blink sketch," which will be explained later. The Pin LED is also used for **debugging**, or fixing the code you have written so that it has no mistakes in it. The **Power LED** is what its name implies: it lights up when the board is receiving power, or is "turned on." This can also be helpful in debugging your code.

There exists on every board the microcontroller itself, called the *ATmega microcontroller*, which is the brain of the entire board. It receives your instructions and acts accordingly. Without this, the entire board would have no functionality.

Analog in pins exist on the opposite edge of the board from the digital pins on the Arduino Uno. It is an input into the Arduino system. *Analog* means that the signal which is being input is not constant, but instead varies with time, such as audio input. In the example of audio input, the auditory input in a room varies with the people in the room talking and with the noises filtering in from outside the room.

GND and *5V pins* are used to create additional power of 5V to the circuit and microcontroller. The *power connector* is on the edge of the Arduino board most often, and it is used to provide power to the microcontroller when it is not plugged into the USB. The *USB port* can be used as a power source as well, but its main function is to *upload*, or transfer, your *sketch*, or set of instructions that you have coded, from your computer to the Arduino.

TX and *RX LED's* are used to indicate that there is a transfer of information occurring. This indication of communication will happen when you upload your sketches from your computer to the Arduino, so they will blink rapidly during the exchange.

The *reset button* is as it sounds: it resets the microcontroller to factory settings and erases any information you have uploaded to the Arduino.

Other Terms about Working with Arduino

There are three types of *memory* in an Arduino system. Memory is the space where information is stored.

Flash memory is where the code for the program that you have written is stored. It is also called the "program space," because it is used for the program automatically when you upload it to the Arduino. This type of memory remains intact when the power is cut off, or when the Arduino is turned off.

SRAM (static random access memory) is the space used by the sketch or program you have created to create, store, and work with information from the input sources to create an output. This type of storage disappears once the power is turned off.

EEPROM is like a tiny a hard-drive that allows the programmer to store information other than the program itself when the Arduino is turned off. There are separate instructions for the EEPROM, for reading, writing to, and erasing, as well as other functions.

Another term that is useful to know is **PWM**, or pulse width modulation. Certain digital pins will be designated as PWM pins, means that they can create analog using digital means. Analog, as we remember, means that an input (or output) is varied and not constant. Normally, digital pins can only create a constant flow of energy. However, PWM pins can vary the "pulse" of energy between 0 and 5 Volts. Certain tasks that you program can only be carried out by PWM pins.

In addition, in comparing microcontroller boards, you will want to look at **clock speed**, which is the speed at which the microcontroller operates. The faster the speed, the more responsive it the board will be, but the more battery or energy it will consume as well.

UART measures the number of serial communication lines the device can handle. **Serial communication lines** are lines that transfer data serially, that is, in a line rather than in parallel or simultaneously. It requires much less hardware to process things serially than in parallel.

Some projects will have you connecting devices to the **Internet of Things**, which essentially describes the interconnectedness of devices other than desktop and laptop computers to various networks in order to share information. Everything from smart refrigerators to smartphones to smart TV's are connected to the Internet of Things.

Chapter 3: Understanding the Choices

Now that we know some basics in understanding the Arduino microcontroller boards, let us look at the various options you have when purchasing an Arduino board. We will look at price, functionality, amount of memory, and other features to help make your decision as easy and straightforward as possible.

Uno

This is the board with which most people start their Arduino journey. It is on the smaller side in terms of memory but is very flexible in functionality and a great tool for beginners and those wanting to try their hand and mind at Arduino. This model has a mini-USB port which allows you to upload directly to the board without using a breakout board or other extra hardware.

Price: $24.95

Flash Memory: 32kB

SRAM: 2kB

EEPROM: 1kB

Processing Speed: 16MHz

Digital Pins: 14 pins

PWM Pins: 6 pins

Analog In: 6 pins

Operating Power: 5V

Input Power: 7-12V

Leonardo

The Leonardo microcontroller board is functional out-of-the-box: all you need is a micro-USB cable and a computer and you can get started. In addition, the computer can recognize the Leonardo as a mouse or a keyboard due to its ATmega32U4 processor.

Price: $19.80

Flash Memory: 32kB

SRAM: 2.5kB

EEPROM: 1kB

Processing Speed: 16MHz

Digital Pins: 20 pins

PWM Pins: 7 pins

Analog In: 12 pins

Operating Power: 5V

Input Power: 7-12V

101

This microcontroller contains a lot of features that are not available in other beginner models. For example, you can connect to the board through Bluetooth Low Energy connectivity from your phone. In addition, it comes with an accelerometer and a gyroscope built in to recognize motion in all directions with its six-axis sensitivity. It can recognize gestures as well.

Put together, these features allow you to have motion of or around the device be the input to which the microcontroller will respond with an output.

Price: $30.00

Flash Memory: 196kB

SRAM: 24kB

EEPROM: 0kB

Processing Speed: 32MHz

Digital Pins: 14 pins

PWM Pins: 4 pins

Analog In: 6 pins

Operating Power: 3.3V

Input Power: 7-12V

Esplora

This board is based on the Leonardo but comes with even more technology built into it so that you do not have to learn as much electronics to get up and running. Instead you can learn as you see the processes work themselves out.

The input sensors that are built in include a joystick, a slider, a temperature sensor, a microphone, an accelerometer, and a light sensor. It also includes some sound and light outputs. It can expand its capabilities by attaching to other technology called a TFT LCD screen through two Tinkerkit input/output connections.

Price: $43.89

Flash Memory: 32kB

SRAM: 2.5kB

EEPROM: 1kB

Processing Speed: 16MHz

Digital Pins: n/a

PWM Pins: n/a

Analog In: n/a

Operating Power: 5V

Input Power: 7-12V

Mega 2560

This microcontroller is designed for larger projects like robotics and 3D printers. It has many times the number of digital pins and analog in pins, as well as almost three times the number of PWM pins. This, along with the many times multiplied flash storage, SRAM, and EEPROM, allows for projects that require more instructions. That is, there is space for greater complexity and specificity in this Arduino board.

Price: $45.95

Flash Memory: 256kB

SRAM: 8kB

EEPROM: 4kB

Processing Speed: 16MHz

Digital Pins: 54 pins

PWM Pins: 15 pins

Analog In: 16 pins

Operating Power: 5V

Input Power: 7-12V

UART: 4 lines

Zero

This is an extension of the Arduino Uno technologies that were developed. It is a 32-bit extension of Uno, and it increases performance with a vastly increased processing speed, 16 times the amount of SRAM and a many times multiplied flash memory. You will pay for the extensions, at almost twice the price of the Uno, but you much more than double your capabilities with this hardware.

One other advantage of the Zero is that it has a built in feature called Atmel's Embedded Debugger, abbreviated as EDBG, which helps you debug your code without using extra hardware and thereby increases your efficiency in the software coding.

Price: $42.90

Flash Memory: 256kB

SRAM: 32kB

EEPROM: n/a

Processing Speed: 48MHz

Digital Pins: 14 pins

PWM Pins: 10 pins

Analog In: 6 pins

Analog Out: 1 pin

Operating Power: 3.3V

Input Power: 7-12V

UART: 2 lines

USB port: 2 micro-USB ports

Due

This is a novelty in the microcontroller board world because it is built on a 32-bit ARM core microcontroller, giving it a great deal of power and functionality. It has an extremely quick processor and 4 UART's, giving it a lot of flexibility and availability to perform multiple functions. It is used for larger scale Arduino projects, and while it might not be you first board, you would do well to consider it for any bigger projects you have down the line.

Price: $37.40

Flash Memory: 512kB

SRAM: 96kB

EEPROM: n/a

Processing Speed: 84MHz

Digital Pins: 54 pins

PWM Pins: 12 pins

Analog In: 12 pins

Analog Out: 2 pins

Operating Power: 3.3V

Input Power: 7-12V

UART: 4 lines

USB ports: 2 micro-USB ports

Mega ADK

This is based on the Mega2560 Arduino board, with incredible memory capacity and a lot of availability for input and output. The difference between the Mega2560 and the Mega ADK is that the Mega ADK is compatible specifically with Android technologies, such as Samsung phones and tablets, Asus technologies, and other non-iOS, non-Windows, mobile devices that use Android. It comes at a hefty almost-$50 price, but if you are looking to incorporate Android into your project, this would be the board with which you would want to do so.

Price: $47.30

Flash Memory: 256kB

SRAM: 8kB

EEPROM: 4kB

Processing Speed: 16MHz

Digital Pins: 54 pins

PWM Pins: 15 pins

Analog In: 16 pins

Operating Power: 5V

Input Power: 7-12V

UART: 4 lines

Arduino Pro (8 MHz)

This is the Sparkfun company's take on the ATmega328 board. It is basically the Uno for professionals and is meant to be semi-permanent in an installation of an object or technology. The 8MHz version is less powerful than the Uno by half, but it is also a good deal cheaper. It requires more knowledge of hardware to get this one working, as it does not have a USB port or way to power the board by USB, and thus must have a connection to an FTDI cable or breakout board to communicate with the board and upload sketches. Once you get through the technicalities of getting this board hooked up to your computer however, it functions like a half-power Uno. Unlike the 16MHz Arduino Pro, this 8MHz Pro can be powered by a lithium battery.

Price: $14.95

Flash Memory: 16kB

SRAM: 1kB

EEPROM: 0.512kB

Processing Speed: 8MHz

Digital Pins: 14 pins

PWM Pins: 6 pins

Analog In: 6 pins

Operating Power: 3.3V

Input Power: 3.35-12V

UART: 1 line

Arduino Pro (16 MHz)

This is the 16MHz version of the Arduino Pro by Sparkfun. It is the same amount of power as the Uno, but has the same drawbacks as the 8MHz Pro: you will need to find a FTDI cable or purchase a breakout board from Sparkfun in order to make the board compatible with your computer to upload sketches. This means learning a *bit* more about the technology than if you were to start with the Uno, but after getting things set up, this will function the same as the Uno.

Price: $14.95

Flash Memory: 32kB

SRAM: 2kB

EEPROM: 1kB

Processing Speed: 16MHz

Digital Pins: 14 pins

PWM Pins: 6 pins

Analog In: 6 pins

Operating Power: 5V

Input Power: 5-12V

UART: 1 line

Arduino M0

This board is an extension of Arduino Uno, giving the Uno the 32-bit power of an ARM Cortex M0 core. This will not be your first board, but it might be your most exciting project. It will allow a creative mind to develop wearable technology, make objects with high tech automation, create yet-unseen robotics, come up with new ideas for the Internet of Things, or many other fantastic projects. This is a powerful extension of the straightforward technology of the Uno, and thus it has the flexibility to become almost anything you could imagine.

Price: $22.00

Flash Memory: 256 kB

SRAM: 32kB

Processing Speed: 48MHz

Digital Pins: 20 pins

PWM Pins: 12 pins

Analog In: 6 pins

Operating Power: 3.3V

Input Power: 5-15V

Arduino M0 Pro

This is the same extended technology of the Uno as the Arduino M0, but it has the added functionality and capability of debugging its own software with the Atmel's Embedded Debugger (EDBG) integrated into the board itself. This creates an interface with the board in which you can debug, or, in other words, a way to interact with the board where you can find the problems in the code you have provided and fix the issues. This would be a good board for you for the same reasons as the M0 would be a good microcontroller for you: it allows for a great amount of creativity while being relatively straightforward like the Uno.

Price: $42.90

Flash Memory: 256 kB

SRAM: 32kB

Processing Speed: 48MHz

Digital Pins: 20 pins

PWM Pins: 12 pins

Analog In: 6 pins

Operating Power: 3.3V

Input Power: 5-15V

Arduino YÚN (based on ATmega32U4)

The Arduino YÚN is a great board to use when connecting to the Internet of Things. It is perfect for if you want to design a device connected to a network, like the Internet or a data network. It has built-in ethernet support, which would give you a wired connection to a network, and WiFi capabilities, allowing you to connect cordlessly to the Internet. The YÚN has a processor that supports Linux code in the operating system, or code language, of Linino OS. This gives it extra power and capabilities but retains the ease of use of Arduino.

Price: $68.20

Flash Memory: 32kB

SRAM: 2.5kB

EEPROM: 1kB

Processing Speed: 16MHz

Digital Pins: 20 pins

PWM Pins: 7 pins

Analog In: 12 pins

Operating Power: 5V

UART: 1 line

Arduino Ethernet

This Arduino board is based on the ATmega328, the same microcontroller as the Arduino Uno. Pins 10 through 13 are reserved to interact with Ethernet, and as such, this board has less input/output capability than the Uno and other Arduino microcontroller boards. It does not connect via USB, but rather through the Ethernet cord, which has the option to also power the microcontroller. There exists on this board, unlike other boards, the option to expand storage through a microSD card reader. The method by which you upload your sketches to this board is similar to the Arduino Pro, and that is via an FTDI USB cable or through an FTDI breakout board. This Arduino model is more complex than a lot of the boards at which we have taken a look, but it has functionalities that are not possible on other boards as well.

Price: $43.89

Flash Memory: 32kB

SRAM: 2kB

EEPROM: 1kB

Processing Speed: 16MHz

Digital Pins: 14 pins

PWM Pins: 4 pins

Analog In: 6 pins

Operating Power: 5V

Input Power: 7-12V

Arduino Tian

The Tian is a miniature computer, with a built-in microprocessor on top of the microcontroller. It has WiFi capabilities like the Arduino YÚN as well as the ethernet capabilities of the YÚN and the Ethernet models. You pay a costly price for the increased functionality and power, but it is many times worth what you pay. This is a fast processor, at 560 MHz clock speed, and on top of it all, this has Bluetooth capabilities. This board also uses the Linino OS, based on the Linux operating system and on OpenWRT.

Price: $95.70

Flash Memory: 256kB (+16MB flash from the microprocessor + 4GB eMMC from the microprocessor)

SRAM: 32kB (+64MB DDR2 RAM from microprocessor)

Processing Speed: 48MIIz (560 MIIz on the microprocessor)

Digital Pins: 20 pins

Analog In: 6 pins

Operating Power: 3.3V

Input Power: 5V

Industrial 101

The Industrial 101 is essentially a small, less capable YÚN for a little more than half the price. It is intended for "product integration," or, in other words, is meant to be used in long-standing projects. It is intended to function in a semi-permanent role within whatever you are building. The board has built-in WiFi capabilities, a USB connection port, and one Ethernet port by which you can connect to networks via Ethernet cord. This board can be connected to your computer via micro-USB in order to upload your sketches for programming.

Price: $38.50

Flash Memory: 16MB on the processor

SRAM: 2.5KB (RAM is 64 MB DDR2 on the processor)

EEPROM: 1kB

Processing Speed: 16MHz (400MHz for the processor)

Digital Pins: 20 pins

PWM Pins: 7 pins

Analog In: 12 pins

Operating Power: 3.3V

Input Power: 5V

Arduino Leonardo ETH

This is the Arduino Leonardo microcontroller board with an Ethernet port to allow the project this uses to extend to the Internet of Things. You can use the Internet to control the sensors in this way, using your own device as a server or signal provider, or as a client, communicating with the microcontroller to receive instructions. This also contains a micro-USB connector to upload your sketches to the flash memory on the Leonardo ETH. This eliminates the need for a breakout board or TKDI cable. Like the Ethernet model of Arduino, this has the option to be powered by the Ethernet cable as well. There is an onboard microSD card reader for extra storage as well. Essentially, this is a powered up Leonardo, with greater flexibility to be used in a wider variety of projects and the capacity to be connected to the Internet of Things.

Price: $43.89

Flash Memory: 32kB (4kB is used by the bootloader, so only 28K available for use)

SRAM: 2.5kB

Processing Speed: 16MHz

Digital Pins: 20 pins

PWM Pins: 7 pins

Analog In: 12 pins

Operating Power: 5V

Input Power: 7-12V

Gemma

This Arduino is made by Adafruit Technologies in the USA. The Arduino Gemma is a miniature microcontroller board that is intended to be worn. It indeed has less space and room for functionality than the non-wearable boards, but for many wearable projects, you will not need the robustness of some of the other Arduino microcontroller boards. There is a micro-USB connection on this board, so you do not need a breakout board or TKDI cable. Instead, you simply upload a sketch via the micro-USB connection and then power the microcontroller by micro-USB or by battery connection.

Price: $9.95

Flash Memory: 8kB

SRAM: 0.5kB

EEPROM: 0.5kB

Processing Speed: 8MHz

Digital Pins: 3 pins

PWM Pins: 2 pins

Analog In: 1 pins

Operating Power: 3.3V

Input Power: 4-16V

Lilypad Arduino USB

This board is round and based on the ATmega32u4 Arduino microcontroller. It contains a micro-USB connected for ease of uploading sketches and for powering the board. There is also a JST connection built in so that, should you decide to power the board by battery, you can do so by connecting a 3.7V Lithium Polymer battery. The difference between the Lilypad Arduino USB and the rest of the Lilypad Arduino models is that the USB model contains the micro-USB port standard, eliminating the need for a breakout board or TKDI adapter. In addition, the board can be seen as a mouse or a keyboard by the computer, among other things.

This board is intended to be worn, like the Gemma. It can be sewn into clothing or otherwise attached to one's body to perform whatever function you have programmed it to perform.

Price: $24.95 (available on Sparkfun)

Flash Memory: 32kB

SRAM: 2.5kB

EEPROM: 1kB

Processing Speed: 8MHz

Digital Pins: 9 pins

PWM Pins: 4 pins

Analog In: 4 pins

Operating Power: 3.3V

Input Power: 3.8-5V

Lilypad Arduino Main Board

This is another wearable Arduino microcontroller board. It can be sewn into a piece of fabric or combined with other sensors, actuators, and a power supply to be something you carry with you with the functionality you have programmed yourself. It requires a breakout board and TKDI cable to upload your sketch to the microcontroller's flash memory, but once you have that piece taken care of, you have an inexpensive, wearable device that you have created yourself.

Price: $19.95 (available on Sparkfun)

Flash Memory: 16kB (2kB are used by the bootloader so only 14kB are available for use by the programmer)

SRAM: 1kB

EEPROM: 0.512kB

Processing Speed: 8MHz

Digital Pins: 14 pins

PWM Pins: 6 pins

Analog In: 6 pins

Operating Power: 2.7-5.5V

Input Power: 2.7-5.5V

Lilypad Arduino Simple

This Arduino microcontroller board model differs from the Lilypad Arduino Main Board in that it possesses only 9 digital input/output pins, about 2/3 the number of pins on the Main Board. This is a good board for simpler projects that do not require as many inputs and outputs. It is also more powerful than the Main Board, having twice the flash memory, SRAM, and EEPROM. This is a powerful, but less functional version of the Lilypad Arduino Main Board, meant to be worn as a transportable device.

Price: $19.95 (available on Sparkfun)

Flash Memory: 32kB

SRAM: 2kB

EEPROM: 1kB

Processing Speed: 8MHz

Digital Pins: 9 pins

PWM Pins: 5 pins

Analog In: 4 pins

Operating Power: 2.7-5.5V

Input Power: 2.7-5.5V

Lilypad Arduino Simple Snap

This is a more expensive version of the Lilypad Arduino Simple and is also designed to create wearable devices and e-textiles. It solves an essential problem of the previous versions: washing the textiles in which is it embedded. With the other models of Lilypad Arduino and with the Gemma, one removes the power source and then hand washes the material in which the microcontroller is embedded or sewn. Then, one must wait for the entire circuity to dry before powering back up, or else a short can happen and ruin the technology.

With the Lilypad Arduino Simple Snap, the 9 pins for input/output are snappable buttons such that the microcontroller board can be removed from the material to which it is initially attached. Then, the material can be washed, and the board is returned to its home on the fabric.

The Lilypad Arduino Simple Snap also has a built-in, lithium polymer battery (LiPo battery), which can be recharged by attaching power to the charging circuit. The way this board is designed, it has the advantage of being able to detach and attach to a new project. You must be careful to attach the snaps in the same way as you would take care in working with the digital pins, but the extra price on this piece of technology might very well be worth it, as you will not be replacing shorted circuity every time you wash that clothing of which the device is a part.

Price: $29.95 (available on Sparkfun)

Flash Memory: 32kB

SRAM: 2kB

EEPROM: 1kB

Processing Speed: 8MHz

Digital Pins: 9 pins

PWM Pins: 5 pins

Analog In: 4 pins

Operating Power: 2.7-5.5V

Input Power: 2.7-5.5V

Other Boards

There exist other boards, like the Arduino Mini, the Pro Mini, the Arduino Robot Control, the Arduino Robot Motor, the Arduino BT, and many others, with the number of options growing quickly.

If you're a beginner, it's recommended that you start with a basic board such as the UNO. Once you're ready for some more advanced projects, these other models might be something you'd like to investigate further!

For now, let us discover how to actually get started with Arduino.

Chapter 4: Choosing and Setting Up the Arduino

The first step in setting up your Arduino microcontroller will be to choose an Arduino board with which you want to work.

Choosing a Board

When looking at the options for Arduino Boards, there are a few factors you will want to consider before making a choice. Before deciding on a board, ask yourself the following questions:

How much power do I need to run the application I have in mind?

You might not know the exact measure of flash memory and processing power that you require for your project, but there is a clear difference between the functioning of a simple nightlight that changes colors, and a robotic hand with many moving parts. The latter would require a more robust Arduino microcontroller board, with faster processing, more flash memory and more SRAM than the more straightforward night light idea.

How many digital and analog pins will I require to have the functionality that I desire?

Again, you need not have an extremely specific idea in mind, but knowing whether you need more pins or less will have a great effect on which board you choose. If you are going for a simple first project, you could get away with having less digital, PWM, and analog pins, while if you are looking to do something more complex, you will want to consider the boards with a great number of pins in general.

Do I want this to be a wearable device?

There are a few options for wearable devices so, of course, this question will not entirely make the decision for you. It will however, help narrow down the choices and steer you in a direction, with Lilypads and the Gemma or other comparable technologies being your best options.

Do I want to connect to the Internet of Things? If so, how?

If you want connectivity to the Internet of Things, your work will be made much easier by the YÚN, the Tian, the Ethernet, the Lenoardo ETH, or the Industrial 101. These have the capabilities of Ethernet connection as well as WiFi capability so you will be able to connect to a network like the Internet and share data or interact with and control other devices on the Internet of Things.

Once you have chosen an Arduino microcontroller board and purchased it, there are a few steps to get yourself set up and ready to go with creating your first program.

Getting Started on Arduino IDE

The Arduino Software runs in an environment called IDE. This means that you will need to either download the desktop IDE to code in, or you will code online on the online IDE.

The first way that you might access IDE, downloading the desktop application, has a few options to suit the various devices that you might be using. First, there is the Windows desktop application. You can also access it from a Windows tablet or Windows phone with the Windows application. Next, there is the Macintosh OSX version, which allows IDE to run on Apple laptops and desktops, but not on Apple mobile devices like iPhones and iPads. Finally, there are three options for running Arduino IDE on Linux: the 32-bit, the 64-bit, and the Linux

ARM version. If you prefer this option to the web browser option, you will simply need to visit the Arduino IDE site by heading to: https://www.arduino.cc/en/Main/Software

There, you can download the appropriate version of desktop IDE. Next, you will run the installation application, click through the options presented, and you should have a running Arduino IDE environment in just a few minutes.

If, on the other hand, you have a stable Internet connection and are not worried about going over a data limit, the web-application is the way to go. This allows you to access the IDE software from Android devices and Apple mobile devices as well, since it is based in a web browser that runs on its own platform rather than on the Android or iOS platforms. You can also run the web browser on various computer types, including Linux, Microsoft Windows and Apple Macintosh. This will allow you to upload your sketches to the Cloud, that is, to store the information you have coded in a secure location that you can then re-access from another device by connection to the Internet.

Coding a Program for Your Arduino

Next you will write code for a program that you want the Arduino board to run. We will cover how to write code for the Arduino boards in the next chapter, but for now let us be sure to understand that the code is written in the IDE on the computer, tablet, or phone, in either the desktop application or the web application. This allows you to see the entire code at once, allowing for easier debugging, or removing of errors.

Once you write the code, you will want to run it and troubleshoot or debug any errors that you find. You will best be able to do this by applying the coded program to the Arduino board and seeing if it runs. To do this, you will need to proceed to the next step of uploading your sketch.

Connecting to the Arduino Board

Some of the boards come with built-in USB, mini-USB, or micro-USB ports. Examples would be the Uno and the Leonardo, for the more beginning stages of your Arduino career. Simply insert the appropriate end of the USB cord into your computer and the other end into the particular USB port that is present on the board you possess, and the Arduino IDE software should recognize the type of board it is. If it does not, you can always choose the correct board from a dropdown menu.

Sometimes you will need to use a TKDI cable or a breakout board in order to make the Arduino compatible with your computer. This means you will insert the TKDI into the TKDI port on the Arduino microcontroller board and then connect it either to your computer or to another board. If you connect the TKDI cable to a breakout board, you will do as you did with the USB-compatible boards: insert the appropriate end of the cord to the breakout board and the other end to the computer. Again, the computer's Arduino IDE software program should recognize your Arduino board, but you can always choose from a dropdown menu should it fail to recognize it.

Uploading to the Arduino Board

To upload your sketch, the program you just created in code, you will need to select the correct board and port to which you would like to upload. It should be easy enough to select the correct board, as you simply look for the board title that matches the name of the type of board you are using.

To select the correct serial port, the options you might choose are as follows:

Mac

Use */dev/tty.usbmodem241* for the Uno, Mega2560 or Leonardo.

Use */dev/tty.usbserial-1B1* for Duemilanove or earlier Arduino boards.

Use */dev/tty.USA19QW1b1P1.1* for anything else connected by a USB-to-serial adapter.

Windows

Use *COM1* or *COM2* for a serial board.

Use *COM4*, *COM5*, or *COM7* or higher for a USB-connected board.

Look in Windows Device Manager to determine which port the device you are using is utilizing.

Linux

Use */dev/ttyACMx* for a serial port.

Use */dev/ttyUSBx* or something like it for a USB port.

Once you have selected the correct board and port, click *Upload* and choose which Sketch to upload from the menu that appears. If you have a newer Arduino board, you will be able to simply upload the new sketch, but with the older boards, you must reset the board before uploading a new sketch, else you will have two, possibly conflicting sketches present in the board's memory, causing it to crash.

The bootloader LED on pin 13 should blink on the board to which you are uploading if everything is working correctly. If not, there will be an error message on your screen.

Running the Arduino with Your Program

There are a few ways to power your Arduino once you have uploaded the program that you have coded to it. First, you can power it by the USB connection to another powered device, such as your computer. Second, you can power by Ethernet on boards with that capability. This means that by connecting to the network, you will be connected to a power source through the Ethernet. Finally, you can power most Arduino's by lithium polymer battery.

Once power is connected and the specified input is put into the microcontroller, it will perform the function for which it is intended.

Chapter 5: Coding for the Arduino

Coding a program for Arduino means learning a new language, but it is not as hard as you might think. In the same way that mathematics has its own set of symbols to denote various functions like addition, subtraction, and multiplication, there are different symbols and terms used when coding for Arduino. Below is a list of the terms and words that are used in Arduino IDE coding and how to use them.

Structure

setup()

This is the function called on when the sketch starts, and will run only once after startup or reset. You can use it to start variables, pin modes, or the use of libraries (specific terms you can download for extra functionality).

loop()

The loop function requires the Arduino microcontroller board to repeat a function multiple times, continuously or until a certain variable or condition is met. You will set the condition for it to stop the loop or you will have it loop continuously until you detach the Arduino from the power source or turn it off.

CONTROL STRUCTURES

If

This that links a condition or input to an output. It means that *if* a certain condition has been met, a specific output or response of the microcontroller will occur. For example, *if* the thermometer to which the microcontroller is attached measures more than 75 degrees Fahrenheit, you might write the code to then direct the Arduino to send a signal to your air conditioning unit to turn on to decrease the temperature back to 75 degrees.

If...Else

This is like the *If* conditional but it specifies another action that the microcontroller will take if the condition for the first action is not met. This gives you an option of performing two different actions in two different circumstances with one piece of code.

While

This is a loop that will continue indefinitely until the expression to which it is connected becomes false. That is, it would perform a certain function until a parameter is met and the statement that is set as the condition is made false.

Do... While

This is like the *while* statement but it always runs at least once because it tests the variable at the end of the function rather than at the beginning.

Break

This is an emergency exit of sorts from a function of the microcontroller. It is used to exit a *do, for,* or *while* loop without meeting the condition that must be met to exit that part of the functionality.

Continue

This is like a *break* in a *loop* or *do, for,* or *while* in that it skips the rest of the iteration of the loop. However, it only does so temporarily until it checks on the condition of the loop, at which point it proceeds with any required additional iterations of the loop.

Return

This is the way to stop a function, and it returns a value with which the function terminated to the calling function, or the function that is asking for the information.

Goto

This piece of code tells the microcontroller to move to another place, not consecutive, in the coded program. It transfers the flow to another place in the program. Its use is generally discouraged by C language programmers, but it can definitely simplify a program.

SYNTAX

; (semicolon)

This is used like a period in the English language: it ends a statement. If you want to be sure that a statement is closed, used the semicolon at the end. Be sure, however, that the statement closed by the semicolon is complete, or else your code will not function properly.

{} (curly braces)

These have many complex functions, but the thing you must know is that when you insert a beginning curly brace, you *must* follow it with an ending curly brace. This is called keeping the braces balanced, and is vital to getting your program working.

// (single-line comment)

If you would like to remind yourself or tell others something about how your code functions, use this code to begin the comment, and make sure that it only takes up one line. This will not transfer to the processor of the microcontroller but rather will live in the code and be a reference to you and anyone who is reading the code manually.

/* */ (multi-line comment)

This type of comment is opened by the /* and it spans more than one line. It can itself contain a single line comment but cannot contain another multi-line comment. Be sure to close the comment with */ or else the rest of your code will be considered a comment and not implemented.

#define

This defines a certain variable as a constant value. It gives a name to that value as a sort of shorthand for that value. These do not take up any memory space on the chip so they can be useful in conserving space. Once the code is compiled, or taken together as a program, the compiler will replace any instance of the constant as the value that is used to define it.

NOTE: This statement does NOT use a semicolon at the end. Do not put a semicolon at the end or you will receive error messages and the program will not function.

#include

This is used to include other libraries in your sketch, that is, to include other words and coding language in your sketch that would not otherwise be included. For example, you could include AVR C libraries or many tools, or pieces of code, from the various C libraries.

NOTE: Do NOT add the semicolon at the end of this statement, just as you would exclude it from the *#define* statement. If you do include a semicolon to close the statement, you will receive error messages and the program will not work.

ARITHMETIC OPERATORS

= (assignment operator)

This assigns a value to a variable and replaces the variable with the assigned value throughout the operation in which it appears. This is different than == which evaluates whether two variables or a variable and a set value are equal. The double equal signs function more like the single equal sign in mathematics and algebra than the single equal sign in the Arduino IDE.

+ (addition)

This does what you might expect it would do: it adds two values, or the value to a variable, or two to a fixed constant. One thing that you must take into account is that there is a maximum for variable values in the C programming languages. This means that, if your variable maxes out at 32,767, then adding 1 to the variable will give you a negative result, -32,768. If you expect that the values will be greater than the absolute maximum value allowable, you can still perform the operations, but you will have to instruct the microcontroller what to do in the case of negative results. In addition, as well as in subtraction, multiplication, and division, you place the resulting variable on the left and the operation to the right of the = or ==.

Also, another thing to keep in mind is that whatever type of data you input into the operation will determine the type of data that is output by the operation. We will look at types of data later, but for example, if you input integers, which are whole numbers, you will receive an answer rounded to the nearest whole number.

- (subtraction)

This operation, like the addition sign, does what you would expect: it subtracts two values from each other, whether they both are variables or one is a constant value. Again, you will have to watch out for values greater than the maximum integer value. Remember to place the resulting variable on the left of the equal sign or signs, and the operation on the right.

* (multiplication)

With multiplication especially, you will need to be careful to define what happens if the value you receive from the operation is greater than the greatest allowable value of a piece of data. This is because multiplication especially grows numbers to large, large values.

/ (division)

Remember to place the resulting variable on the left of the operation, and the values that you are dividing on the right side of the operation.

% (modulo)

This operation gives you the remainder when an integer is divided by another integer. For example, if you did $y = 7 \% 5$, the result for y would be 2, since 5 goes into seven once and leaves a remainder of 2. Remember, you must use integer values for this type of operation.

Comparison Operators

== (equal to)

This operator checks to see if the data on the left side of the double equal signs matches the data on the right side, that is, whether they are equal. For example, you might ask the pin attached to the temperature gauge $t == 75$, and if the temperature is exactly 75 degrees, then the microcontroller will perform a certain task, whether it be turning off the heating or cooling, or turning off a fan.

!= (not equal to)

This is the mirror image of the previous operation. You could just as easily write a program to test $t != 75$ and set up the microcontroller to turn on a heating lamp, turn on a fan, or ignite the wood in the fireplace if this statement is true. Between == and !=, you can cover all the possible conditions that input might give your microcontroller.

< (less than)

This is a simple operation that mirrors what it does in mathematics and algebra: it tests whether a value is less than another value. If this statement is true, then you can program a certain response from your microcontroller, or, in other words, program an output for such input.

> (greater than)

This operation test is one value on the left is greater than the value on the right. If the value on the left is equal to or less than the value on the right, the statement becomes false. Only in cases where the value on the left is greater than the value on the right will your true statement response of the microcontroller be triggered.

<= (less than or equal to)

This is a similar comparison operator to the less than operator, but it becomes a false statement *only* when the value to the left is greater than the value on the right. This means that <= is the absolute opposite of >. For example, if $x <= y$ is true, then $x > y$ is necessarily false.

>= (greater than or equal to)

The greater than or equal to statement only becomes false if the value on the left is less than the value on the right. Greater than or equal to has an absolute opposite as well, the less than. *If a >= b is true, whether a is greater than b or a is equal to b, then a < b is necessarily false.*

Variables

CONSTANTS

HIGH

This value is different based on whether the pin is set up as an input or an output. Should the pin be an input, it will read HIGH if:

1) A voltage greater than 3.0V is present on a 5V board

   OR

2) A voltage greater than 2.0V is present on a 3.3V board.

If the pin is set up as an output, it will output as follows:

1) It will output 5V from a 5V board

   OR

2) It will output 3.3V from a 3.3V board.

LOW

This value is different based on whether the pin is set up as an input or and output. Should the pin be an input, it will read LOW if:

1) A voltage less than 1.5V is present on a 5V board

OR

2) A voltage greater than 1.0V is present on a 3.3V board.

If the pin is set up as an output, it will output as follows:

1) It will output 0V from a 5V board

AND, similarly,

2) It will output 0V from a 3.3V board.

INPUT

In the input state, a digital pin will require very little of the processing power and energy from the microcontroller and battery. Instead, it is simply measuring and indicating to the microcontroller its measurements. The rest of the work is done by the microcontroller and the output pins.

OUTPUT

These are very good at powering LED's because they are in a low-impedance state, meaning they let energy flow freely through them without much resistance. Output pins take their directions from the microcontroller once it has processed the information given by the input pins, and the output pins power whatever mechanism will perform the intended task.

INPUT_PULLUP

This is what mode you will want to use when connected to a button or a switch. There is a lot of resistance involved in the INPUT_PULLUP state. This means that it is best used for Boolean-like situations, such as a switch either being on or off. When there are only two states and not much in between, use INPUT_PULLUP.

LED_BUILTTIN

This code references and calls on the built-in LED. It is useful for debugging your work. The built-in LED is connected to pin 13 on most boards.

true

In a Boolean sense, any integer that is not zero is true. 1 is true, 200 is true, -3 is true, etc. This would be the case when a statement matches reality. One of your pins might be testing a value, and the statement is it trying to match is $y \mathrel{!}= 35$, so if the pin receives information that the value of y is 25, then the statement $25 \mathrel{!}= 35$ is true.

false

This is part of a Boolean Constant, meaning that a statement is false, or that its logic does not match reality. For example, you could have a statement, $x > 7$ and the value the microcontroller receives for x is 3. This would make the statement *false*. It would then be defined as 0 (zero).

integer constants

These are constants that are used by the sketch directly and are in base 10 form, or integer form. You can change the form that the integer constants are written in by preceding the integer with a special notation signifying binary notation (base 2), octal notation (base 8), or hexadecimal notation (base 16), for example.

floating point constants

These save space in the program by creating a shorthand for a long number in scientific notation. Each time the floating point constant appears, it is evaluated at the value that you dictate in your code.

DATA TYPES

Void

This is used in a function declaration to tell the microcontroller that no information is expected to be returned with this function. For example, you would use it with the *setup()* or *loop()* functions.

Boolean

Boolean data holds one of two values: true or false. This could be true of any of the arithmetic operator functions or of other functions. You will use *&&* if you want two conditions to be true simultaneously for the Boolean to be true, || if you want one of two conditions to be met, either one setting off the output response, and ! for not true, meaning that if the operator is *not* true, then the Boolean is true.

Char

This is a character, such as a letter. It also has a numeric value, such that you can perform arithmetic functions on letters and characters. If you want to use characters literally, you will use a single quote for a single character, 'A' and a double quote for multiple characters, "ABC" such that all characters are enclosed in quotes. This means the microcontroller will output these characters verbatim if the given conditions are met. The numbers -128 to 127 are used to signify various signed characters.

Unsigned Char

This is the same as a character but uses the numbers 0 to 255 to signify characters instead of the "signed" characters which include negatives. This is the same as the byte datatype.

Byte

This type of data stores a number from 0 to 255 in an 8-bit system of binary numbers. For example, B10010 is the number 18, because this uses a base 2 system.

Int

Integers are how you will store numbers for the most part. Because most Arduinos have a 16-bit system, the minimum value is -32,768 and maximum value of an integer is 32,767. The Arduino Due and a few other boards work on a 32-bit system, and thus can carry integers ranging from -2,147,483,648 to 2,147,483,647. Remember these numbers when you are attempting arithmetic with your program, as any numbers higher or lower than these values will cause errors in your code.

Unsigned Int

An unsigned integer frees up the 16th bit in the 16-bit system since the first bit is no longer being used as a positive or negative sign. This yields the ability to store numbers from 0 to 65,535 on the 8-bit boards with which you will likely be working. If you have higher values than the signed integers will allow, you can switch to unsigned integers and achieve the same amount of range but all in the positive realm, such that you have a higher absolute value of range.

Word

A word stores a 16-bit unsigned number on the Uno and on other boards with which you will likely be working. In using the Due and the Zero, you will be storing 32-bit numbers using words. Word is essentially the means by which integers and numbers are stored.

Long

If you need to store longer numbers, you can access 4-byte storage, or 32-bit storage in other words, using the long variable. You simply follow an integer in your coded math with the capital letter *L*. This will achieve numbers from -2,147,483,648 to 2,147,483,647.

Unsigned Long

The way to achieve the largest numbers possible and store the largest integers possible is to direct the microcontroller using the unsigned long variables. This also gives you 32 bits or 4 bytes to work with, but being unsigned, the 32nd bit is freed from indicating the positive or negative sign in order to give you access to numbers from 0 to 4,294,967,295.

Short

This is simply another way of indicating a 16-bit datatype. On every type of Arduino, you can use short to indicate you are expecting or using integers from -32,768 to 32,767. This helps free up space on your Due or Zero by not wasting space on 0's for a small number and by halving the number of bits used to store that number.

Float

A float number is a single digit followed by 6 to 7 decimal places, multiplied by 10 to a power up to 38. This can be used to store more precise numbers or just larger numbers. Float numbers take a lot more processing power to calculate and work with, and they only have 6 to 7 decimals of precision, so they are not useful in all cases. Many programmers actually try to convert as much float math to integer math as possible to speed up the processing. In addition, these take 32 bits to store versus the normal 16 bits, so if you're running low on storage, try converting your float numbers to integers.

Double

This is only truly relevant to the Due, in which doubling allows for double the precision of a float number. For all other Arduino boards, the floating point number always takes up 32 bits, so floating does nothing to increase precision or accuracy.

Functions

DIGITAL I/O

pinMode()

This is the notation you will use to set a pin's mode, whether it be INPUT, OUTPUT, or INPUT_PULLUP. The syntax you will use is:

pinMode(pin#, mode)

such that setting analog pin 5 to INPUT would look like this:

pinMode(A5, INPUT)

digitalWrite()

This will write a HIGH or LOW value to a digital pin. You will write:

digitalWrite(HIGH)

OR

digitalWrite(LOW).

This will tell the pin whether to allow the maximum voltage through and into the connected LED or device, or to shut off and not let any current through, essentially turning the device or LED off.

digitalRead()

This is a way to read the data that is measured by a certain or specific pin. It reads HIGH or LOW. The syntax used is:

digitalRead(pin#)

such that if you want to read the measurements from pin 3, you would write the code:

digitalRead(3).

ANALOG I/O

analogRead()

This will read the information being fed into the specific analog pin that you choose and map out the results versus time, with integer values between 0 and 1023. This is a 10-bit analog to digital converter, and hence the numbers you can read will be between the minimum of 0 and the maximum of 1023. It can read as many as 10,000 times per second.

The syntax for this is as you might expect, such that reading analog pin A4, you would write:

analogRead(A4)

analogWrite() – PWM

This will use one of the PWM pins, since the analog pins are specifically for input. It can use the information from an *analogRead* function to create a response. For example, it can change the speed of a motor or brightness of an LED. The values of the *analogWrite* function are between 0 and 255, so to get an allowable number from the 0 to 1023 *analogRead* function, you will need to divide by 4, to make the range between 0 and 255.

Here is an example:

```
void loop()
{
  val = analogRead(analogPin);
```

```
analogWrite(ledPin, val / 4);
}
```

This code will allow you to see in the brightness of the LED how quickly a wheel is turning or some other varying input value.

Chapter 6: Projects with the Arduino

There are many different projects that you might try once you have your Arduino board. The boards and Arduino IDE come with a few pre-made sketches that you can try and then manipulate in order to figure out how the components of the code work.

Once you have played around for a while with the out-of-the-box sketches like Blink, you can move onto more challenging projects where you can create something useful or intriguing. For example, you might create a Smart Phone Garage Door Opener, a Talking Clock, or an alarm that tells you when you have intruders. You could build a thermostat or an LED stoplight as well, or you can mimic a heartbeat with LED blinks on the Arduino board itself. If you like to play games with dice, you can create an automated dice roller too.

Different projects will require different Arduino models, and as such you'll want to find projects suitable to your Arduino model, as well as to your experience in coding. Fortunately, the code for thousands of Arduino projects are available for free online. Due to its open source nature, people are free to create, share, and alter the way their Arduinos operate, and the functions that they perform. This has created a great community in which people make their code and project details available for free!

Several websites that include some of the most popular Arduino projects for free are as follows:

- https://www.hackster.io/arduino/projects

- http://www.electroschematics.com/arduino/

- http://www.electronicshub.org/arduino-project-ideas/

Your best bet would be to head to those websites and begin with some beginner programs that look interesting to you. The code is already provided in a simple format, where you can copy it straight into the IDE. This is much more practical than manually typing out the code line by line, as you would do if following the instructions for a program written in this book. You can make changes to programs as you wish, especially as you get more comfortable with using the Arduino.

To simply give you an example within this book of what the code looks like for an Arduino program, we've included a couple of sample projects in this chapter for you.

LCD RGB Shaded Glasses

For this project, you will need:

PCB

68 X WS2812 LEDs

68 X 100nF 0805 Capacitors

An Arduino microcontroller, preferably a smaller model

3 pin male header

External power source (ie: a power bank)

Cables to connect the Shades to the power source and to the Arduino

Instructions

1. The first thing you might want to do is test all of the LEDs, since they will be running serially, one bad LED will ruin the entire line of current and cause the entire thing to malfunction or not function at all.

2. Now, solder the capacitors in place and the LED's overtop. You might break LEDs in the process, so be sure to pick up a few spare while you're out purchasing them.

3. Next, connect the port called S on the Shades to the 3rd pin, Pin 3, on your Arduino. GND must then be connected to GND of the external power supply and to the GND of the Arduino, using the 3 pin male header. Finally, in this step, connect the VCC to the +5V external power supply. MAKE SURE YOU DO NOT EXCEED THE VOLTAGE indicated by the Arduino, or you will destroy the circuitry.

4. You will now use the code below, playing with it to make it your own, in order to create a color distribution that you like. Make sure to read the comments in the code, marked at the beginning of a single line comment by // and a multi-line comment starting with /* and ending with */.

CODE

```
#include "FastLED.h"

// How many leds in your strip?
#define NUM_LEDS 68

byte pixelType = 0;
byte drawIn[4];
byte frameIn[NUM_LEDS*3];


// For led chips like Neopixels, which have a data line, ground,
and power, you just
// need to define DATA_PIN.  For led chipsets that are SPI
based (four wires - data, clock,
// ground, and power), like the LPD8806 define both
DATA_PIN and CLOCK_PIN
#define DATA_PIN 3
//#define CLOCK_PIN 13

// The bluetooth module pins
#define RX_PIN 0
#define TX_PIN 1
```

```cpp
// Define the array of leds
CRGB leds[NUM_LEDS];

void setup() {
  // Uncomment/edit one of the following lines for your leds
arrangement.
  // FastLED.addLeds<TM1803, DATA_PIN, RGB>(leds,
NUM_LEDS);
  // FastLED.addLeds<TM1804, DATA_PIN, RGB>(leds,
NUM_LEDS);
  // FastLED.addLeds<TM1809, DATA_PIN, RGB>(leds,
NUM_LEDS);
  // FastLED.addLeds<WS2811, DATA_PIN, RGB>(leds,
NUM_LEDS);
  // FastLED.addLeds<WS2812, DATA_PIN, RGB>(leds,
NUM_LEDS);
  FastLED.addLeds<WS2812B, DATA_PIN, GRB>(leds,
NUM_LEDS);
  // FastLED.addLeds<NEOPIXEL, DATA_PIN>(leds,
NUM_LEDS);
  // FastLED.addLeds<APA104, DATA_PIN, RGB>(leds,
NUM_LEDS);
  // FastLED.addLeds<UCS1903, DATA_PIN, RGB>(leds,
NUM_LEDS);
  // FastLED.addLeds<UCS1903B, DATA_PIN, RGB>(leds,
NUM_LEDS);
  // FastLED.addLeds<GW6205, DATA_PIN, RGB>(leds,
NUM_LEDS);
  // FastLED.addLeds<GW6205_400, DATA_PIN, RGB>(leds,
NUM_LEDS);

  // FastLED.addLeds<WS2801, RGB>(leds, NUM_LEDS);
  // FastLED.addLeds<SM16716, RGB>(leds, NUM_LEDS);
  // FastLED.addLeds<LPD8806, RGB>(leds, NUM_LEDS);
  // FastLED.addLeds<P9813, RGB>(leds, NUM_LEDS);
  // FastLED.addLeds<APA102, RGB>(leds, NUM_LEDS);
  // FastLED.addLeds<DOTSTAR, RGB>(leds, NUM_LEDS);

  // FastLED.addLeds<WS2801, DATA_PIN, CLOCK_PIN,
RGB>(leds, NUM_LEDS);
```

```cpp
  // FastLED.addLeds<SM16716, DATA_PIN, CLOCK_PIN,
RGB>(leds, NUM_LEDS);
  // FastLED.addLeds<LPD8806, DATA_PIN, CLOCK_PIN,
RGB>(leds, NUM_LEDS);
  // FastLED.addLeds<P9813, DATA_PIN, CLOCK_PIN,
RGB>(leds, NUM_LEDS);
  // FastLED.addLeds<APA102, DATA_PIN, CLOCK_PIN,
RGB>(leds, NUM_LEDS);
  // FastLED.addLeds<DOTSTAR, DATA_PIN, CLOCK_PIN,
RGB>(leds, NUM_LEDS);
  Serial.begin(9600);

  pinMode(TX_PIN, OUTPUT);
  pinMode(RX_PIN, INPUT);
}

void loop() {

}

void serialEvent() {
  pixelType = Serial.read();

  switch (pixelType) {
   case 0:
   //draw mode
     while (!Serial.available()) {}
     Serial.readBytes(drawIn, 4);

     leds[drawIn[0]] = CRGB(drawIn[1], drawIn[2], drawIn[3]);

     FastLED.show();
     Serial.flush();
     break;

   case 1:
     //clear mode
     for (int i = 0; i < NUM_LEDS; i++)
     {
       leds[i] = CRGB::Black;
     }
```

```
    FastLED.show();
    Serial.flush();
    break;

  case 2:
  //frame in mode
    while (!Serial.available()) {}
    Serial.readBytes(frameIn, (NUM_LEDS * 3));
    for (int i = 0; i < NUM_LEDS; i++)
    {
      leds[i] = CRGB(frameIn[i * 3], frameIn[(i * 3) + 1],
frameIn[(i * 3) + 2]);
    }

    FastLED.show();
    Serial.flush();
    break;

  case 3:
    while (!Serial.available()) {}
    int brightnessLED = Serial.read();
    FastLED.setBrightness(brightnessLED);
    Serial.flush();

    break;
  }
}
```

5.   Once you have the code to your liking, you can create the Arduino sketch file, or .ino file, and upload it to your Arduino microcontroller board. Then it's just a matter of plugging it into the power source and you will have you LED RGB Shades working!

Smart Doorbell

Many times, we find that we miss someone when they stop by, whether because we are not home or even because we do not hear them knock on the door. Here is a solution that will tell you when someone rings your doorbell, notifying you by smartphone message through the application, Blynk, which works on both Android and iOS, and by email if you desire.

The materials you will need for this project include:

An Arduino Uno

Breakout board

Jumper wires

Push button doorbell

Ethernet shield

Blynk application

Instructions

1. First connect the push button to the breakout board.

2. Then connect the ethernet shield to the board so that the push button is connected to network capability.

3. Next, upload the following sketch, inserting your own messages and email address into the code that follows:

```
#define BLYNK_PRINT Serial
#include <SPI.h>
#include <Ethernet.h>
#include <BlynkSimpleEthernet.h>
#include <SimpleTimer.h>

// You should get Auth Token in the Blynk App.
// Go to the Project Settings (nut icon).
char auth[] = "YourAuthToken";
```

```
SimpleTimer timer;

WidgetLCD lcd(V1);

void setup()
{
  Serial.begin(9600);
  Blynk.begin(auth);

  while (Blynk.connect() == false) {
    // Wait until connected
  }
}
void notifyOnButtonPress()
{
  // Invert state, since button is "Active LOW"
  int isButtonPressed = !digitalRead(2);
  if (isButtonPressed) {
    BLYNK_LOG("Button is pressed.");

    Blynk.notify("Please open up! Somebody is on the door!");
    lcd.clear(); //Use it to clear the LCD Widget
    lcd.print(4, 0, "Open"); // use: (position X: 0-15, position Y: 0-
1, "Message you want to print")
    lcd.print(4, 1, "The Door!");
  }
}

void emailOnButtonPress()
{

  int isButtonPressed = !digitalRead(2); // Invert state, since
button is "Active LOW"

  if (isButtonPressed) // You can write any condition to trigger e-
mail sending
  {
    BLYNK_LOG("Button is pressed."); // This can be seen in the
Serial Monitor
```

```
    Blynk.email("youremail@address.com", "Subject: Doorbell",
"Please open up! Somebody is on the door!");
    lcd.clear(); //Use it to clear the LCD Widget
  lcd.print(4, 0, "Open"); // use: (position X: 0-15, position Y: 0-
1, "Message you want to print")
  lcd.print(4, 1, "The Door!");

  }
}

void loop() {
  // put your main code here, to run repeatedly:
  Blynk.run();
  timer.run();
}
```

4.   Finally, connect the Arduino board to the breakout
board such that the push button is connected to the input
pin and the output pin is connected to the power line.

Some High Level Uses for Arduino

Over the years, Arduino has been used for numerous, extremely
useful purposes. For example, Arduino technologies feature in
Ardupilot, a drone software and hardware, as well as in
OBDunio, a technology used in some cars to report speed and
other various measurements. Arduino is used to lower costs of
virtual reality technologies and comes into play heavily in C-
STEM Studio to teach hands-on integration of computing,
science, technology, engineering, and mathematics through the
use of robotics.

Gameduino uses Arduino technology to recreate retro 2-D
games like Snake and other early videogames. ArduinoPhone is
a cell phone that you can create yourself too. Arduino can be
used to test water quality, detect when cow milk goes bad, and is
useful in automatic titration systems.

A Word of Encouragement

You might be just a beginner in the Arduino world, but your creativity could make a true difference in someone's life, whether it be your own or the life of someone else.

It might be that you have found this book self-explanatory, in which case you are well on your way to using Arduino professionally. Even if you do not yet have a clear grasp yet of Arduino, this technology is intended to help the average person become more knowledgeable in computing. Like any skill, this will take some practice, but it will be well worth your effort, whether to entertain yourself, your family and friends, or to benefit the world at large.

Conclusion

Thanks again for taking the time to read this book!

You should now have a good understanding of Arduino, and be ready to get started on your first projects!

If you enjoyed this book, please take the time to leave me a review on Amazon. I appreciate your honest feedback, and it really helps me to continue producing high quality books.